Seriously

WHAT ARE YOU WAITING FOR?

13 ACTIONS TO IGNITE YOUR LIFE
& ACHIEVE THE ULTIMATE COMEBACK

TAMIKA FELDER

To request Tamika Felder to speak at your organization or event, please contact events@tamikafelder.com.

ISBN-13: 978-0-9992134-0-7

Tamika Felder International, LLC
Upper Marlboro, MD 20772
U.S.A
2017

Dedication

For my parents, TJ and Mary Ann. They are the greatest source of my desire to excel. They grew up with nothing and catapulted their lives to succeed beyond their circumstances. They loved me unconditionally and made me sweet as pie, yet tough as bricks. I can't quit, because they never quit on me. I am who I am today because of their love and sacrifice. They are missed with every breath that I take. I thank them for this solid foundation upon which I stand.

"*This book will light the fire in you. There have been peaks and valleys in my life when I have been trying to figure out my purpose. During those times, Tamika has been a source of inspiration and encouragement. She pushed me to see the potential I have for greatness.*"

−Kenya Hughes

"*For more than a decade, I saw firsthand how Tamika motivated, comforted and empowered countless people facing life's most difficult challenges with her irresistible combination of bold honesty and southern charm. We worked in close quarters as television producers in Washington, DC and before long, I too grew to depend on her advice, which was always given frankly but with so much love and humor that I began to believe in my own potential. The experience transformed me and helped me find my life's ambition. I am delighted that this book will help so many others discover their own potential.*"

−Cecily Fernandez

"*Very powerful, uplifting, and inspirational. This book has something that all can relate to and identify with. This book is the perfect tool and guide to get you to the next level.*"

−Corey Moorer

"*Engaging and interactive book which really helps with setting priorities and attaining goals. Tamika's words continue to transform me from cancer thriver to advocate and really impact my life for the better.*"

−Erica Frazier Stum

"*If we wait until we're ready, we'll be waiting for the rest of our lives.*"

–Lemony Snicket

Contents

"If you want to grow and develop yourself, embrace failure. If you want to become the best at what you do, you've got to be willing to fail, again and again. And then finally, one day, you can fail your way to greatness."

–Les Brown

Intro

This book is for you, you and you! Seriously, this book has something for everyone. My story to finding happiness came after surviving the death of both of my parents, my father when I was 16 and my mother when I was 33. It came after surviving my own cancer diagnosis at 25. It came after understanding who I am, what I want and what I will and won't allow in my life. I have to tell you that it's a beautiful thing - to know who you are, your worth and your purpose. Together, those things create a beautiful, wonderful and bountiful life.

What I've noticed most from people that I encounter is that they have a general idea of what they want to do, but they don't know how to get there. They run around in circles and then eventually give up and stew about it. They get stuck and they don't know how to move forward or deviate from the plan slightly to get back on track. It's very cliché, but anything worth having takes lots of elbow grease, patience and passion. It's easy to allow the voices in your head to tell you that you are not good enough, or that you missed your window of opportunity or that there are other factors in life that are more important and your true passion should take a backseat. I couldn't disagree more. There is no time like the present. Whether you are a cancer survivor trying to get your life back, an entrepreneur who doesn't know how to showcase your talent, a student who has a wicked side hustle that you are trying to get off the ground, or a person just trying to find your footing and the right direction, this book is for you.

If you're looking for clarity and there is a voice inside of your head that's telling you to not give up, then you've taken the first step in getting there. In this book, I will give you tips on how to move forward and a place to create your own master blueprint for your life. And, guess what? It's all stuff you already know. You just have to believe in yourself and *make it happen*. I know, I know — easier said than done. But if you really want this, YOU will do the work. Because, *seriously, what are you waiting for*?

I used to ask myself that question a lot. There were always a ton of reasons holding me back from walking in my purpose. Family responsibilities. I was no longer a spring chicken. I had adult things, like a mortgage, car note, and insurance. I had a great paying job that I was *supposed* to be thankful for (and I was).

All of those things and more kept me in a holding pattern. And on top of it, I was miserable! But instead of twiddling my thumbs and dreaming about what I could have been, I created my plan and worked on my great escape from the things in life that brought me no joy and kept me away from the things I most wanted. *Freedom, happiness, world travel*, and a chance to *make a difference*. Everything in this book comes from everything that I've experienced, what it taught me, how I reacted and most importantly, how I moved *forward*. It's real life. So let's get started. Live, learn and soar!

Tamika

300

I am obsessed with the movie 300. If you have seen it, you know what I'm talking about! If not, download it, rent it, and watch it as soon as you can. It is the story of a small Spartan army that takes on the massive Persian hordes and their egotistical, maniacal and delusional King who is threatening to enslave them. These Spartans are not having it and they are not going down without a fight. They don't care that they are outnumbered.

They will fight until the death for Sparta (and they do!). Here's the thing — it's all real (well, mostly real). You know how Hollywood dramatizes things. But it's based on a true story. 300 is my go-to movie to get me fired up and ready to conquer anything. I watch that movie and I beat on my chest, I pump my fist in the air and I'm ready to go to battle. Sure, it may be just a proposal or pitch for a new gig, but whatever — the details don't matter. You get my point.

Go and get this movie and keep it in your arsenal of items that get you hyped and ready to conquer any and everything. It's epic!

Here are a few of my favorite quotes, my interpreted takeaways from the movie and how they apply to everyday life.

Messenger: "Choose your next words carefully"

Persian: A thousand nations of the Persian empire will descend upon you. Our arrows will blot out the sun!
Stelios: Then we will fight in the shade.

This is Self-explanatory!

[Dilios is putting a patch over his eye]
King Leonidas: Dilios, I trust that "scratch" hasn't made you useless.
Dilios: Hardly, my lord, it's just an eye. The gods saw fit to grace me with a spare.

Never make excuses. Never. There is always a workaround.

Dilios: Immortals... we put their name to the test.

Again, no excuses.

Queen Gorgo: Freedom isn't free at all, that it comes with the highest of costs. The cost of blood.

People will try you. Prepare to backup your name and talent.

Dilios: We did what we were trained to do, what we were bred to do, what we were born to do!

Well, if this isn't the truth. Your freedom from whatever is holding you back will cost you blood, sweat and tears.

Know your sh*t.

4

Ephialtes: *My father trained me to feel no fear, to make spear and shield and sword as much a part of me as my own beating heart!*

Be fearless and walk like a boss.

King Leonidas: *Children, gather round! No retreat, no surrender; that is Spartan law. And by Spartan law we will stand and fight... and die. A new age has begun. An age of freedom, and all will know, that 300 Spartans gave their last breath to defend it!*

Don't give up. Never, ever give up.

And, my absolute favorite…

King Leonidas: *Give them nothing! But take from them everything!*

Let your light shine. Stop making yourself small. Stand firm in your true talent and light. Be bold and daring. It's okay to shine bright!

300 (2006.) USA: Warner Bros.

5

Firestarter

We all have experiences that define the trajectory of our lives. A loss, a medical issue, an accident, an attack or even something as small as a statement or conversation. A lot of the examples I use in this book will reflect my cancer survivorship, loss of my parents, and the feeling of being stuck in a dead end job. It's okay if you haven't experienced any of those things. Simply use whatever you've gone through to help catapult you into your next chapter.

There was this time I was at a dinner and a woman came up to me after I spoke on a panel and inquired about my happiness. I wasn't shocked by this at all. It's actually something that I am asked about regularly. But there was something about the sheer amazement of her questioning. She wanted to know if I was always "this happy" and if so, how I became that way. She really looked at me as if she was staring at a unicorn or something! On the panel, I shared about all of my hardships in life, including the loss of my parents and my cancer diagnosis and how I never thought I would have survived them. It really resonated with this woman, as she shared with me her own loss and how there were things that have happened since the loss that brought her joy, but that she's never been truly happy since experiencing her loss. She wanted to know what was my secret to be being so happy, despite everything that I've been through.

The truth is: My happiness comes easy for me because **I choose to be happy.** There is no other way for me. It's a decision that I purposely decided on and I actively work to be the happiest person I can be. Sounds crazy, right? When my mother was alive, I often remember her saying to me at various times in my life, *"You are such a happy person. I hope you always stay that way."* When she died, I wasn't prepared at all. It seemingly came out of nowhere and honestly, a part of me died with her — or so I thought. I thought because I had experienced my father's death decades before, I would know how to deal with my mother's death. I knew that it would be painful, but I would learn how to cope and move on without hearing her voice every single day - yes, we spoke every single day. So, why am I talking so much about death in a book that's about happiness? Because my near death experience and the death of my parents helped to catapult me to my happiness. It also started a fire within me to live my best life. It gave me a greater understanding that we all will leave this earth. Death is the one thing that will happen and in most cases, we won't know when or how it will happen. If reincarnation exists, we surely won't come back as the same being. So just to be safe, this is the life we have to succeed at, and success comes in many different forms. There is a monetary success and then there is a peace, a sort of joy that comes with knowing that you are where you are supposed to be, doing *exactly what you should be doing* and living life like you want.

This book is a workbook. So grab your favorite writing utensil and let's get to work! Throughout this workbook, there will be lots of questions. Don't let them overwhelm you. These questions will help you gain clarity and get focused on your goals. These are the same tools that I used to create a visual plan for my life. More importantly, it's how I ignited my life. And how do you start a fire? A real fire starts with kindling.

kindling
/'kindlin/

noun

small sticks or twigs used
for lighting fires.

a process by which a seizure or
other brain event is both initiated
and its recurrence made more likely.

What is your kindling? What small steps will you take to get started on your journey to the life you want to live? For me, it was mapping out what I wanted to do with my life — professionally and personally. This is what you will use to build the foundation of your blueprint and to keep you balanced as you find clarity in your life. The point of this exercise is to know what you want. You can't move forward until you know what goals you want to attain.

Top 3 Goals For Your Personal Life

1._____

2._____

3._____

Top 3 Goals for Your Professional Life

1._____

2._____

3._____

Now describe what makes you happy. If you had no responsibilities, what are the things you would do with your time? For this, imagine that money isn't an obstacle and you could do whatever you wanted, whenever you wanted. To put it simply, what would you do if you weren't afraid?

_____

_____

_____

_____

_____

_____

_____

Do not skip ahead. This is really important. If you have to walk away and think about it, that's fine. But this is a very important step. In life, we tend to want to put the cart before the horse. In most cases, it won't work! Things don't need to be perfect, but you do have to start and you do have to do the work.

The Lucky 13

So now that you have your goals, let's start thinking about life and how to eliminate or put up barriers to the things that keep you from moving forward. I've found strength in following a few simple life rules I learned along my journey.

When I celebrated 13 years of cancer survivorship — something I never thought I would — I shared a blog post, "13 Ways I Now Live My Life With Purpose After Cancer." What I found is that anyone can relate to these action steps -- not just cancer survivors. They are things we all learn over time, with age, through life experiences. These "Lucky 13" are the ways I live my life with purpose every day.

11

Action #1 : No longer sweat the small stuff.

I know just how short life can be. Therefore, I don't want to waste time on things (or people!) that really don't matter. Have you ever had someone in your life that really just annoyed the crap out of you? You know, the type of person who could suck the air out of an entire room and not give a crap about it?

What about when things happen in your life that really set you off...for what seems like an eternity? I remember a time when something would happen to me, like a co-worker who tried to undermine me during a staff meeting. I would get myself so upset over the situation; it was all I would talk about and it would just take so much energy and time to shake it off. Of course, when we are in the midst of it happening, we never think of it as a "small thing." These emotional roller coasters tend to come into our space like tornadoes, and leave an aftermath of destruction in their wake.

After facing death, you learn that time is important. So, I don't waste time on things that are not important. In life, you have to be careful what you give energy to. Learn to shift any negative energy out of you and your space. It takes practice and patience, but you can do it. As you develop your knack for shifting your energy, you will notice that things, especially small trivial things, won't bother you in the same way. I'm not saying that there won't be things or people that get under your skin, but take action to no longer sweat the small stuff and you will have better coping mechanisms to move past them when they come at you.

"Do not bring people in your life who weigh you down. And trust your instincts ... good relationships feel good. They feel right. They don't hurt. They're not painful. That's not just with somebody you want to marry, but it's with the friends that you choose. It's with the people you surround yourselves with."

–Michelle Obama

Good-Bye Energy Vampires!

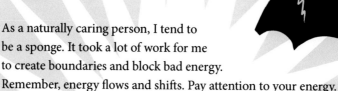

As a naturally caring person, I tend to
be a sponge. It took a lot of work for me
to create boundaries and block bad energy.
Remember, energy flows and shifts. Pay attention to your energy.

Have you ever noticed that certain people you encounter change
your mood? Those are your energy vampires. Recognize them and
keep them at bay. There is no time or place in your life for energy
vampires. They transfer their energy to you and then you are both
miserable. You can't save energy vampires. So don't even try!

Sweating the small stuff includes any draining obligations you're
hanging onto. You know what I'm talking about - the things that
you don't want to do. For me, it was housekeeping. Having a
clean organized home was a priority for me, but I just couldn't do it.
I've never enjoyed cleaning and really don't think I'm that good at it!
So, I hired someone to clean my home - I reworked my household
budget and allotted a portion for a housekeeper. Sure, I can do small
upkeep. But deep cleaning my house, it's just not my focus and it
sucks my energy. When you are building an empire or a movement,
you can't be or do everything. I proudly proclaim that I am not
every woman!

Who are the people, places and things that suck all of your energy?

Now is the time to start taking control of the energy that you allow into your space.

Decide your time and energy priorities. Jot them down here in this space.

_____

_____

_____

_____

_____

_____

_____

_____

_____

_____

Now, what are the "small things" you're sweating that are keeping you from dedicating time to those priorities?

_____

_____

_____

_____

_____

_____

_____

_____

_____

What tools will you create to keep you focused on your priorities, and how will you manage your time to do so?

_____

_____

_____

_____

_____

_____

_____

_____

_____

*"When people show you who
they are, believe them."*

−Maya Angelou

Action #2 : **Cherish the people who really matter to you.**

Why is it so hard for us to believe what we see? For me, I want to see the good in everyone. But the truth is that everyone won't be your friend. They won't want to see you succeed and they will keep you from moving forward. Now, I'm not talking about your supportive clique. I'm talking about the double-handed comments clique. The "Why would you want to do that?" clique. You know, the "keep you from soaring" clique. Evaluate the people in your circle(s). Just like you spring clean your house, sometimes you need to clean out the people who shouldn't have a say, comment or expression on how you live.

Cancer taught me who my true friends were. As a result, my circle became much smaller. That annoying friend that you're always ducking... just cut them loose. That family member that makes you so uncomfortable...you may not be able to cut them loose, but you can cut them back... seriously, way back! Your time is precious. Choose to spend it with people who matter.

I know! You can't believe that I said to cut off a family member! Shocking! I had a family member who always gave me crap about weight, even when I was a little girl. I loved her and she loved me but I always felt bad about myself when she was around. As I got older, I started limiting my time with her. She would always say the same thing to me whenever she would see me. "You're just getting bigger and bigger, huh?" I remember being a teenager and the pain and the anger I felt. It didn't matter what I did in my life; this particular family member only saw me for the bigger body I had. But on the flip side, I had family members and friends who made me feel incredible about myself. I'm sure they're a big part of my having such huge self-awareness and confidence. These friends and family members are also people who matter to me. They are the people that I want to share my wins with and I know that they will clap for me. They are also the people when I am at my lowest that I seek out to help pick me up again.

"Surround yourself with CHEER leaders
NOT FEAR leaders."

–Karen Salmansohn

The people you want in your life are the ones who have your back - the types you can count on when this world seems too tough. They are your personal cheering squad. I tell people: "To have good friends, you have to be a good friend (or a good family member)." Cherish those people, and let them know they matter to you. In this technology-filled world, a card or a personal written note can go a long way.

When my mother was alive, I used to randomly send her a dollar or two and tell her to have a Snickers bar on me. She had a (secret) wicked sweet tooth, and that was one of the small ways I showed her that I cared. I would even address the card to "The Best Mother In the Whole Wide World." When my mother died, the mailman told me that he always got a kick out of delivering my notes to my mother.

Give people their flowers while they are living. Make sure that you show your love and cherish the people who matter most to you. Sometimes, I get so focused in my work that I shut out most of the world, and sometimes those closest to me fall through the cracks. I'm learning to make time for those that I cherish. I used to send "thinking of you" cards all the time. As my time became limited, so did those small gestures. I'm working on rekindling gestures. While rebuilding my life after cancer, I may not always have time, but I am trying my best to let those that I love know that they matter to me - that even when I'm not physically there, I am thinking of them.

A ship is designed to take you to places. So, if your *friend*SHIP, *partner*SHIP, *companion*SHIP or *relation*SHIP isn't taking you anywhere… abandon SHIP!

Seriously, who are your cheerleaders? The people who encourage you and lift you up and empower you to keep going?

_____

_____

_____

_____

_____

_____

_____

_____

_____

_____

What type of information and personalities do you let influence your spirit — even from social media? Those personalities impact your life whether you realize it or not. If you surround yourself with positive, purpose-filled people, you will think positively and purposefully. The saying is true: _Birds of a feather flock together_. Who's in your flock?

_____

_____

_____

_____

_____

_____

_____

_____

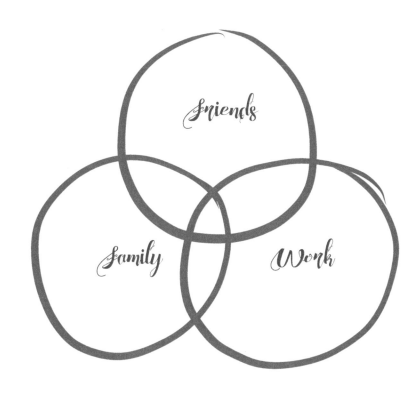

How do the above circles impact your life? What do you give to them and what do you receive from them?

_____

_____

_____

_____

_____

_____

_____

_____

Do people in your circles like the idea of you, and what you can do for them? Or, do they like you for you, and the joy you bring to their lives?

_____
_____
_____
_____
_____
_____
_____
_____
_____

How are you fed from the relationships around you? No, I'm not talking about the dinner table! I mean emotionally fed.

_____
_____
_____
_____
_____
_____
_____
_____
_____

Relationships can have expiration dates. Be honest with yourself when they have expired. Everyone is not meant to go with you on your journey. If it doesn't feel right or make you happy, let that relationship go and move on.

I am the type of person who always wants closure. I have to not only have an ending, but an ending that I understand. I need for it to make sense. Cancer taught me that sometimes, it's more important to let go of what is holding me back, rather than waiting for a "closure moment" that never comes. It was so freeing to let go of that desire. There will not always be closure, but freedom is always available to you if you have the courage to let go.

Think about who you cherish most. List them below.

_____

_____

_____

_____

_____

_____

_____

_____

_____

How will you cherish those that matter most?

_____

_____

_____

_____

_____

_____

_____

_____

_____

Action #3: **Love the skin you're in.**

For the longest time, I yearned for my life before cancer. The truth is that I am no longer that person. After feeling in limbo for so long, I finally heard the message coming through, loud and clear: "Embrace the new you. It just might surprise you!"

When I was much younger, I remember standing in the bathroom curling my hair, with one of those 80's cordless butane curling irons. I probably was in there too long, and my sister came in and just stood there looking at me. Out of nowhere, she told me to always be proud of myself and to love myself. I just kind of said, "Okay," as most teens would do. She went on and told me if I was going to be "that size" (read: 'big'), that there was nothing wrong with it, and that I should always take care and pride myself in the way that I dress and look— and I always have.

Our society would have you think that if you are not wrapped in this perfect marketing ad of a body that you are not pretty. That you are not worthy and that there is something wrong with you. I've never bought into that. I've always had a pretty high self-esteem, but that doesn't mean that it comes all from looks. I have confidence because of my ability to love myself — all of me, all of my parts.

Of course, we all have moments when we don't like things about ourselves. We wish we could be taller, thinner, etc. It's a list that could go on and on!

We need to love ourselves more. No, I'm not talking about a bunch of self-absorbed people running around doing self-PDAs! What I mean is, seeing your flaws and still loving them because they are a part of you. Every stretch mark, booty dimple and saggy belly.

I was hanging out with a few girlfriends and somehow or another we got on the topic of physical beauty. We were celebrating one of our friend's latest accomplishments and started taking photos. One of my beautiful friends shared that she no longer liked taking photos because she didn't like how she looked. It broke my heart. My friend is not only physically beautiful but she is internally beautiful. She complained about all the weight that she had gained and the changes that come with aging.

I get it. I see so many differences in my current physical appearance — the silver hairs, the sagging skin, and the new aches and pains that seemingly appear overnight with each waking day. But one thing that I do know for sure is that change means that I am still here. Aging is a gift. It is not something that everyone is fortunate enough to experience. We have to learn to be truly happy with ourselves and truly love the skin that we are in — and work to change the things that we don't. Life is too short to be unhappy. The one struggle that I have always had is my weight. But through it all, I've loved myself and I continue to love myself. It doesn't mean that I believe we should all be overweight and unhealthy. Just the opposite. I think we should be happy and healthy and love the skin we are in.

So yet again, I'm on a path to be the healthiest that I can be. Not the skinniest, but the healthiest. Whatever size that may be.

Self-care is a very important part of taking care of oneself. Not only for releasing negative energy and having a reset, but as a reminder to love yourself.

What do you do to take care of yourself? What is your self care plan? If you do not have one, now is a great time to write down a few ideas.

_____

_____

_____

_____

_____

_____

_____

_____

_____

Action #4 : **Stop living in the past.**

I believe everything that has happened in my life has prepared me for where I am today and where I am going tomorrow. The *good*, the *bad* and the *ugly*.

Don't let what's happened in the past keep you from living. I have an acquaintance in the cancer community that I see on a regular basis and she is so afraid to live. She lives in fear, constantly, always waiting for cancer to reemerge. I get it. I really do. But those of us who are still here are blessed to be alive, no matter the physical or emotional limitations. So live... *like never before*.

Often, I'm asked, "How do I keep going and not throw in the towel?" I don't know if it's being the baby of the family and being spoiled rotten, or knowing what my parents sacrificed for me to thrive. Or maybe it's all of that, plus knowing (not telling myself, but actually knowing) that *I am not built to quit*. Perhaps my resilience is because all of the obstacles I had to overcome at a young age: my father's death, my own cancer diagnosis, the loss of my fertility, my mother's death and a supervisor who tried to ruin my career. Those things impacted me. They took me to low places, but I never gave up on myself. I came pretty darn close, but there is something within me that just won't let me quit. I'm simply not built for it. I am a constant work in progress. I'm always striving to be better than the day before.

I know too many people who experience a loss, tragedy or some impactful event that they can't recover from. Something that leaves them emotionally and physically paralyzed. It's very easy to stay stuck. But what kind of life is that? This is the time to dig deep and get centered. Lean on your tribe and get back to living.

What from your past is holding you hostage?

_____

_____

_____

_____

_____

_____

_____

_____

_____

How will you release yourself from your hurtful past?

_____

_____

_____

_____

_____

_____

_____

_____

_____

"Do the one thing you think you cannot do.
Fail at it.
Try again.
Do better the second time.
The only people who never tumble are those who never mount the high wire.
This is your moment.
Own it."

–Oprah Winfrey

Action #5 : **Enjoy life.**

Prior to cancer, I hardly ever took vacations. Typically, I would take one weekend in the summer and another extended weekend at Christmas. I never thought I had enough time, money or a break in the workload. You have to rest and reset. All work and no play... you know the rest!

How do you enjoy life?

_____

_____

_____

_____

_____

_____

_____

When you hit the reset button, how will you spend your time? Think hard and include the time, place, and people you will spend it with.

_____

_____

_____

_____

_____

_____

_____

Action #6 : Dance (and sing!) like no one is watching.

It's okay to be silly and happy. Just go ahead and do it. It's good for your soul. My niece, Linyah, is a great mom - partly because she is a big kid herself! It's something that we have in common. I love watching her with her children. As a family, they're always on some adventure or doing something outrageously fun - the kind of fun that makes the best childhood memories.

One of the things that she does so well is that she takes her children outside to play in the rain. I never did that as a child. I mean, I've gotten caught plenty of times in the pouring rain, but I've never purposely chosen to go outside and run wild and free in the rain and stomp around in water puddles. I'm sure it's because I never wanted to ruin my hair. Fast forward to my wedding day - it was beautiful, a true fairy tale and my dream come true. But it rained. And rained. And rained. Did I mention that it was an outdoor wedding? But that night, I didn't care about ruining my hair. I let it all go and danced in the rain and sang at the top of my off-key lungs. All night long.

That experience taught me a valuable lesson. To this day, I can't truly put into words the euphoric pleasure I experienced, just by giving myself the permission to be free and happy, on this, the most important day of my life. Imagine if we could do that every day, how powerful we could be. Because of that experience, I'm not afraid to dash out in the rain and dance and romp around, just because!

*"Death is a tragic thing
if you haven't lived."*
–Charlotte Cartwright

Film: The Family That Preys by Tyler Perry

So, just dance. Right now (Yes, I mean right now), I want you to get up and just DANCE. You don't even need music. Then, come back and write down how it made you feel to let go! Bonus points for dancing in the rain!

_____

_____

_____

_____

_____

_____

_____

_____

_____

_____

"Always do your best.
What you plant now,
you will harvest later."

–Og Mandino

Action # 7 : Let go of what's holding you back.

When you are faced with mortality, you start thinking of all the things that are left unaccomplished or need a do-over. Sometimes you have to learn to let those things go. For me, it was finally realizing that a certain level of my career would never be obtained. I fought it for years, but the truth is that I'm so much more passionate about different things now. My priorities have completely changed. So, I let it go. I made a new, more up-to-date list of goals, and I am going for it.

When I decided to quit my secure and cushy job, it wasn't an overnight decision. In fact, it took a lot of prayer and number-crunching. Though it was scary, what I found was that I was more than ready. This was a season of change that I had been planning (or planting, as Og Mandino would say!) for quite some time. With any significant change, there comes worry, fear and doubt. But those feelings are normal and essential. It's what you do when those feelings come into play that are most important. You have to push through. You have to keep going and work through the emotions.

Change is like a roller coaster. It can be scary because it takes you out of your comfort zone. You're terrified just waiting to begin. Then you finally get on, and it's still scary. You're up, twisted from side to side. You're down, back and forth, and then it happens all over again. AND THEN you make it to the end of the ride, and it was exhilarating, right? So much so that you wondered why you waited so long!

I'm hanging onto that feeling... you know, the one at the end of the ride. That great feeling of accomplishment, so powerful that it makes you want to go through it all over again. But you can't know that feeling of fulfillment unless you get on the ride in the first place. So be open to change. Go into it knowing that it can be a difficult adjustment, but it can bring a beautiful reward.

I've been planting and tending to "this" for a very long time.
It's harvest time.

Change is scary. **Growth** is hard. But remember, you only have to have faith the size of a mustard seed to light that fire within you. Seriously, what are you waiting for?

33

Change can be hard but it's almost always inevitable.

In life, you should always experience change, because life is about evolving. You should be on a path to constantly learn new things and reach higher places in your life. It's called growth. And without change, there is no growth.

God, the universe, a totem, whatever it is that you believe in will keep you centered and will always give you what you need. You just have to stop and listen. There truly are signs everywhere.

I climbed part of the Great Wall of China. Yes, me. The woman with this big and heavy body! If you've ever been, you know just walking up to the entrance is all uphill. I was gasping for air just from that. While in China, I was with someone who taunted me about my weight the entire trip. I remember her telling me that the Great Wall included a lot of uphill walking and then looking at me in that way that said, *"Tamika, it's not something you can do."* But I couldn't go to Beijing and NOT see the Great Wall. You're probably also aware by now that I've also always been that type of person who just has to try something, even when it seems impossible. So, I did. And it was hard. Not as hard as cancer, but it was very challenging. I had to keep stopping, and up on that mountain, as I took yet another break, I started worrying about the trip back down. Just as I became overcome with worry and doubt that I could make it, I was surrounded by a cloud of beautiful butterflies. To me, it was a sign that I could, and a reminder that we sometimes have to get out of our comfort zones in order to get to the next level. Getting to the next level means that we sometimes have to morph. And metamorphosis only happens when we let go and accept change without fighting it.

Like a caterpillar, I have emerged from my cocoon transformed.

LIFE comes with an expiration date. It's morbid but true. There is no more "putting it off until tomorrow." Tomorrow is not promised. Do it now. I'm not saying go crazy, but what I am saying is that none of us are getting out alive. The time to live your life is now.

There is a line in the film *The Family That Preys* by Tyler Perry where the matriarch's character, played by the great Alfre Woodard, asks the question, "Are you *Living* or *Existing*?"

It's a pretty powerful question. Are you living or existing? Say it out loud. Let that set in for a moment. Do you have your answer?

Right now, ask yourself…
Who am I?

_____

_____

_____

_____

_____

_____

_____

_____

_____

What is my purpose in life?

_____
_____
_____
_____
_____
_____
_____
_____
_____
_____

What am I passionate about?

_____
_____
_____
_____
_____
_____
_____
_____
_____
_____

What/who makes me happy?

_____

_____

_____

_____

_____

_____

What/who makes me unhappy?

_____

_____

_____

_____

_____

_____

"You can't build your life on hurts from the past."
−Alice Evans

Film: The Family That Preys by Tyler Perry

What's holding me back from the life I want?

_____
_____
_____
_____
_____
_____
_____
_____
_____
_____

How do I navigate past the obstacles holding me back?

_____
_____
_____
_____
_____
_____
_____
_____
_____

When I feel discouraged, how will I continue to manifest and ignite what I am passionate about?

_____

_____

_____

_____

_____

_____

_____

_____

_____

Action # 8 : **Enjoy every little morsel.**

I enjoy everything. Seriously. Every bite of food, drink, kiss from my hubby... everything! You don't know when a moment's going to be your last, so savor it.

Years ago, there was a woman in my life who died after a long illness. She lived to a ripe old age, and her death wasn't a surprise. But she was the type of person who always waited for the 'perfect' opportunity to use the good china, wear the expensive jewelry, or drink the perfectly aged wine. When I thought of the time I'd spent with her, I realized she was always waiting. When she died, her special things that she was waiting for the perfect time to use were gifted out to family and friends. She had missed the opportunity to enjoy her beautiful, special things.

What I want you to realize is that "the perfect time" is now. When I almost died from cancer, there was a shift that happened in me. I got it - that realization that tomorrow was not promised. Right then and there, I started drinking and eating off of the "good" china and crystal. I was no longer waiting for holidays or special occasions — now was the time to enjoy all of the wonderful things in life.

It's not just the good china, either. Take the time to enjoy simple things like lounging in the hammock in the backyard. In this fast-paced life, we are always in a constant state of rushing. We are like the hamster on the hamster wheel. Sometimes, you just need to jump and believe that your feet will plant firmly on the ground.

What are the things you want to enjoy?

_____

_____

_____

_____

_____

_____

_____

_____

_____

What will it take for you to commit more time to enjoy these things?

_____

_____

_____

_____

_____

_____

_____

_____

_____

_____

SET YOUR
SOUL ON FIRE.
Seek Those Who
Fan Your Flames.

-Rumi

Action # 9 : **Be adventurous.**

Do things that scare the crap out of you. Why? Because they remind you
that you're still here. Since surviving cervical cancer, I've traveled around the
world alone (I have a slight fear of long plane rides); I've taken a toboggan
down the Great Wall of China (I had to climb it first); I've learned how to
swim (something that's very hard to learn to do as an adult); I rode an
African Elephant (it's very scary and unsteady up there); and I took a chance
on love (yay, for love!) and all of its endless possibilities.

What's on your bucket list?

What's holding you back from experiencing the things on your bucket list?

_____

_____

_____

_____

_____

_____

_____

_____

_____

_____

How will you make it happen?

_____

_____

_____

_____

_____

_____

_____

_____

_____

_____

Action # 10 : **It's OK to reflect.**

You can't truly appreciate how far you've come unless you look back on where you've been. But remember, it's just a reflection. Don't let looking back at the past consume you. We've all had struggles and challenges. No matter how small or large, these are the things in life that propel us. They make us soar. Because of our struggles, we all have a story to tell about how we became the person that we are or will be.

What's your backstory?

_____

_____

_____

_____

_____

_____

_____

_____

_____

_____

This story will be the story that you tell yourself over and over again, and it will do one of two things. It will either **1)** catapult you to your next chapter and be the thing that you rejoice and marvel at how you overcame it or **2)** it will hold you hostage, keeping you stuck and miserable.

What will your story do for you? Which number will you let it be - #1 or #2?

_____

_____

_____

_____

_____

_____

_____

_____

_____

_____

Note: if you find yourself veering towards **number 2**, make a *way*, not an *excuse*, to get to **number 1**. Go ahead. You can do it. Why? Because FREE-DOM is the sweetest word. HOSTAGE is not!

I left my career as a television producer because I was held hostage by it. No, I'm not being dramatic. I was physically, emotionally, and mentally held hostage by my job! I was in a no-win situation, and at the time, I thought it was because of a particular person. After true reflection, it was simply because it wasn't for me anymore. I had overstayed my time. Sure, I had cancer, so that increased my time there. My mother died, and I stayed longer. Catastrophic things for sure kept me imprisoned because I needed my insurance,

I was depressed, and it wasn't time for a major change. **THE TRUTH** was this, though: I had outgrown the job, office and people. But I stayed because of one thing: fear. I'm going to say something. If you are offended by *colorful* language, quickly divert your eyes to the next paragraph!

*FEAR IS A MOTHERF*CKER!*
It is paralyzing!

FEAR is the demonic voice in your head that tells you that you CAN'T. That you WON'T. That this is it. There is nothing more. That's fear.

It's time for you to close the door on fear and be FEARLESS.

Prior to my cancer diagnosis, I thought I was fearless. I thought I was invincible and could do anything. There were no limitations. I stood up for myself, my wants and my desires. I was one of those kids that wanted to be so many things. My mother wanted me to become a teacher. She grew up during a time when there weren't many choices for women — especially, black women — and teaching was an honest, good and attainable career choice. There's nothing wrong with becoming a teacher, but it wasn't for me. Why? Because it wasn't what I wanted to do. When I told my mother I wanted to work in television production, she was so upset. She didn't understand.

In truth, it wasn't for her to understand. The small liberal arts school I attended didn't even have a program in television production - only English with a concentration in Mass Communications! But I had a dream, and that was enough for me. I jumped on it, selected it as my major, and soared. In so many ways, I am a teacher, just not in the way my Mom wanted me to be. Cancer was what truly made me fearless. It made me realize that I could die at 25 and there was much that I still wanted to do. It took time, but I found my way. Deep down, it was that desire to live - to truly live my life in a way that I had always desired.

Most of the things that we want out of life are NOT unattainable. In fact, it mostly takes passion, a plan, and the execution of said plan. But you have to acknowledge that there are no perfect plans and things won't always go as you plan! It's okay to yield when you approach forks in the road of life. The point is to not stall. Just keep moving forward.

What is that desire deep in your gut? Is it something from childhood, or a new vision for your life that seems unachievable?

SELF-PITY
I never saw a wild thing sorry for itself.
A small bird will drop frozen dead
from a bough without ever having felt
sorry for itself.

–D. H. Lawrence

Action # 11 : **Have a pity party.**

What happened to you was messed up. Maybe your dream job fell through, or the love of your life decided to call it quits after a lifetime of togetherness. Doesn't matter whether it's Stage 0 or Stage 4 -- cancer is not fun. A loss of a loved one leaves an unexplainable void. A career disappointment can be crushing. What I disliked most when going through something was when someone would tell me to just "get over it." Often, it's not so easy. There is a necessary grieving process. So take time to be sad, to accept the blow you've been dealt. But remember - you have to move on and fight for your life, because it's going to take everything you've got - mentally and physically. It doesn't matter whether it's an illness, loss or major change - don't lose yourself in the midst of it.

"Just Keep Swimming."

−Dory from Finding Nemo

What are you dealing with that has you stuck?

_____

_____

_____

_____

_____

_____

_____

_____

_____

How will you get yourself unstuck? What's your plan?

_____

_____

_____

_____

_____

_____

_____

_____

_____

*"The best way to find
yourself is to lose yourself
in service of others."*

–Mahatma Gandhi

$\mathcal{Action}$ # 12 : **Give back.**

Volunteer, give financially, get involved! There are so many amazing organizations out there, especially the smaller grassroots movements that would love your time, money, or energy. Use the scenarios below to find a path to give back and make a difference. Feel free to create one based upon your own situation.

Think about what you needed while you were going through treatment. What would have made a difference to you? Go back to your cancer center and make it happen. Recruit friends and family.

_____

_____

_____

_____

_____

_____

_____

_____

_____

_____

Visit Cervivor.org to see how I give back.

Think about what would have made a difference for you after a loss of a loved one. What did you or your family need most? How could the load have been lightened?

_____

_____

_____

_____

_____

_____

_____

_____

Is there a career center where you can coach young professionals or those returning to the workforce?

_____

_____

_____

_____

_____

_____

_____

_____

_____

How would you like to give back? Perhaps it's a pie drive during the holidays. Or giving out blankets to the homeless. We are so lucky even if we don't have much. It's more than some. How will you make a difference in this world? What will your charitable legacy be?

_____

_____

_____

_____

_____

_____

_____

_____

_____

_____

_____

_____

Action #13 : **Be happy.**

You are ALIVE! So go and be happy. As I mentioned earlier, my mother would often say to me, "You are always so happy. I hope you stay that way." So I make it a point to be just that - happy! Don't get me wrong - I still am human. There are times when I find myself sad, angry or just plain unhappy. It is in those moments that I remember that I am still here and I don't want to waste a moment being unhappy.

What makes you happy?

_____

_____

_____

_____

_____

_____

_____

_____

_____

_____

_____

_____

_____

_____

When something gets under your skin and you can't shake it, what coping skills will you use to get you back to your happy place?

_____

_____

_____

_____

_____

_____

_____

_____

_____

_____

_____

_____

_____

_____

_____

If today was your last day, would you be happy with the legacy that you are leaving behind? I'm not talking about world peace, or a remedy for the ozone layer depletion. You could do those things, but what is your realistic goal for making a difference? My legacy is something that I never thought, sprinkled with something that I always did. Sounds a little crazy, but basically, it is my blended love of storytelling and cancer advocacy. I am so much more fulfilled because I know my "why."

What will your legacy be?

_____

_____

_____

_____

_____

_____

_____

_____

_____

_____

_____

_____

_____

_____

Your legacy is YOUR legacy. Stop trying to keep up with the Joneses!

How do you measure success? My idea of success is not how much money I have in the bank. Money is great but at the end of the day, my success is measured by the way I live my life, the people's lives that I impact, and the legacy I will leave when I am gone.

I thought I wanted the nice car, the fancy house, and you know - the picket fence! And, there is nothing wrong with those things. But, I knew early on those things weren't the *only* things for me. Society tells you that you have to get married. You have to have kids. You have to have the perfect storybook life. You know what I realized? It's okay to have the life that *you* want — whether it includes those things or not. It's also important to accept that the life we imagined doesn't always come easy.

Disney Princesses for example, always have some adversity before they get to their happily ever after. Have you noticed that? It's never easy. So why do we think life should be easy for us? Life is not a fairy tale. It's filled with twists, U-turns and surprises. You just have to keep holding on and remember to BREATHE.

Light The Match!

You've been waiting and waiting. For what? Perfection? It's never going to be perfect. There, I said it! There is no perfect time. The time is **now**. MAKE IT HAPPEN NOW. Tomorrow is not promised. No, I'm not saying slap something together. I'm saying **stop waiting and procrastinating.** You are not a tree. You can get up and move at any time, even when you feel weighed down. Taking the first step is the hardest step. Take it and keep the momentum going. It's the only way you will begin.

Now what? It's time to soar.
Live your life. Not someone else's life,
but your life. Your beautiful, glorious
life, filled with all its hiccups, failures,
and unbelievable wins. Go ahead and
live your imperfectly perfect life.
I dare you!

Spark

There
is a spark in you
that can't be extinguished.
Only you know what that is and only
you can fan the flames and allow it to grow.
Now that you have a bit more clarity about what
you want to do and where you want to go, it's time
for you to connect with like-minded people.

Think about your circle and if it needs to be rebooted.
Remember, people have seasons and reasons in
your life. Identify and accept them. Negative
and unsupportive people will be the first to
extinguish your spark — don't let them.
You got this!

*The biggest adventure you
can take is to live
the life of your dreams.*

–Oprah Winfrey

Seriously,
what are YOU waiting for?

Tamika

Photo by Lakisha Matthews

Tamika Felder is in love with life and all of
its endless possibilities. When she's not out
sharing her story, she can be found living her
rules for life with her husband and stepdaughter.
They split their time between Maryland and
Tamika's family home in the lowcountry of
South Carolina.

Acknowledgements

I am thankful for life and all of its lessons. Everything in life is a lesson, whether you acknowledge it or not. I've learned and grown from all my highs and especially, the lows. I'm thankful to my tribe of family, friends, mentors, and world changing do-gooders. You inspire me and keep me climbing up that mountain called life. Thank you.

Amanda Miller Littlejohn, you are an amazing business coach and friend. You have lit a fire in me that can't be extinguished. Thank you. I'd also like to recognize my friend and book coach, April Capil. She kept me on a schedule even though I fell off hard at times. Good thing she was always there with an encouraging word and revised schedule. Thank you for keeping me on task. I couldn't have completed this without you. If you're going to write a book, you have to have a thorough editor. Thankfully, I didn't have to look far. Thank you to my friend and editor extraordinaire, Helaine Bader. Also, my sister, Valildra Berry, my first reader, who always tells it like it is and loved it from page one. And, to Iman Newsome for your continued support in every aspect of my life.

I'd be remiss without thanking all the patients, survivors and friends who allow me into their lives. This book would be nothing without all of our talks and sessions — especially, Curtissa Clay, my Cervivor sister and friend. You filled my cup up so much that Sunday afternoon in San Diego at Cervivor School. You encouraged me and pushed me to complete this. You may not be physically here, but you are always here. I miss you and I thank you.

Curtissa Clay
1973 - 2016

Finally, I have to end by giving thanks to my family. They are the real MVPs. My husband, Rocky, who gets me and doesn't ever make me choose. My stepdaughter, Zakiya, because she constantly would ask, "When are you going to finish your book?" There is nothing like a teenager keeping you in check and encouraging you to complete your goal. Thank you. I love you both.

Wow, I wrote a book. Look Zakiya, I finished it! What's next?

Let's get social!

Connect With Me:

 /seriouslytamika

 @tamikafelder

 @tamikafelder

 /tamikafelder

 /tamikafelder

#SeriouslyTamika

Notes

Notes

Made in the USA
Monee, IL
27 September 2019